Flags
Of The
World

Denise Santoro

AuthorHouse™
1663 Liberty Drive
Bloomington, IN 47403
www.authorhouse.com
Phone: 833-262-8899

Because of the dynamic nature of the Internet, any web addresses or links contained in this book may have changed
since publication and may no longer be valid. The views expressed in this work are solely those of the author and do
not necessarily reflect the views of the publisher, and the publisher hereby disclaims any responsibility for them.

Any people depicted in stock imagery provided by Getty Images are models,
and such images are being used for illustrative purposes only.
Certain stock imagery © Getty Images.

This book is printed on acid-free paper.

ISBN: 978-1-6655-5009-3 (sc)
ISBN: 978-1-6655-5010-9 (e)

Print information available on the last page.

Published by AuthorHouse 03/02/2022

authorHOUSE®

Thank you!

To all good black and white people of the United States of America throughout the world, we would like to thank you for keeping us safe. But now I need everyone to writing a bill voting it into law, First offense 5 to $25,000 cash. Second offense 5 to 10 years in prison. Third offense the electric chair.

Are writing it in on your balance sheet. Black men can be fathers their children, husband to their wives, a friend to a friend, black mothers can be mother to her children, and other children that needs a mother.

And the boys and girls can get the skills and trades to have a good education learning environment learning their history. I'm not asking much. We are living human beings.

Abkhazia

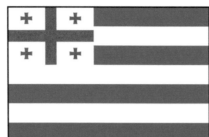

Adjara

Adygea

Afghanistan

African Union

Ainu

Aland Iceland

Albania

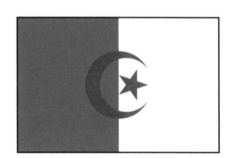

Algeria

Amazigh

American Samoa

Andorra

Flags Of The World

Angola

Anguilla

Anishinaabe

Antarctica

Antigua and Barbuda

Arab League

Arapaho

Argentina

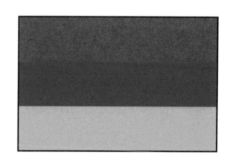

Armenia

Artsakh

Aruba

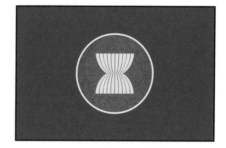

ASEAN

Flags Of The World

Ascension Island
Australia
Austral Islands

Austria
Azerbaijan
Azores

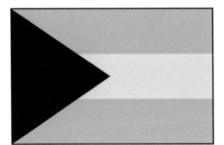

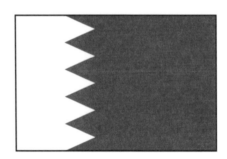

Bahamas
Bahrain
Balochistan

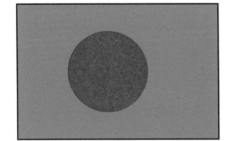

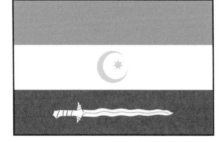

Bangladesh
Bangsamoro
Barbados

Flags Of The World

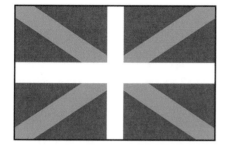

Basque Country

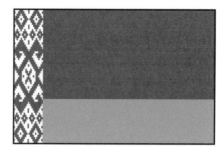

Belarus

Belgium

Belize

Benelux

Bermuda

Benin

Bhutan

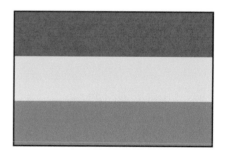

Bolivia

Bolivia

Bonaire

Bosnia and Herzegovina

Flags Of The World

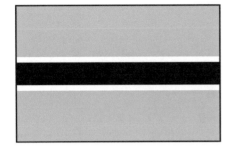

Botswana

Bougainville

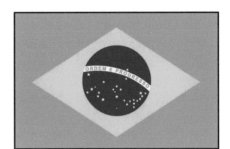

Brazil

British Virgin
Islands

British Indian
Ocean Territory

Brittany

Brunei

Bulgaria

Burkina Faso

Burundi

Cambodia

Cameroon

Flags Of The World

Canada

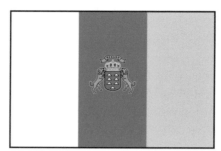

Canary Islands

Cape Verde

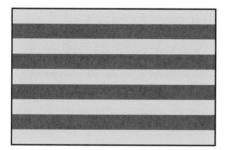

Catalonia

Cayman Islands

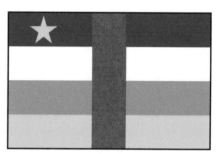

Central African
Republic

Ceuta

Chad

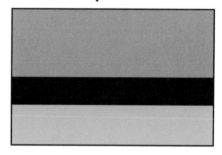

Chagos Islands

Chatham Islands

Chechnya

Chile

Flags Of The World

China

Christmas Island

Chuuk

CIS

Cocos Keeling Islands

Colombia

Comoros

Congo

Cook Islands

Corsica

Costa Rica

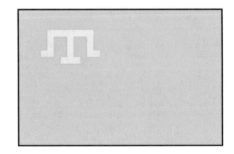

Crimean Tatar

Flags Of The World

Croatia

Cuba

Curacao

Cyprus

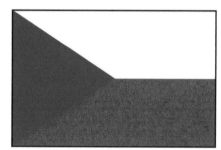

Czech Republic

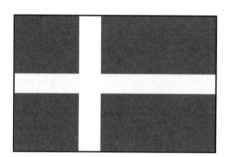

Denmark

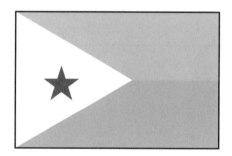

Djibouti

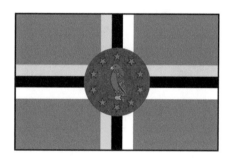

Dominica

Dominican Republic

Donetsk Republic

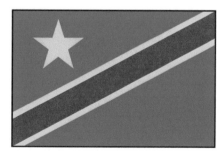

DR Congo

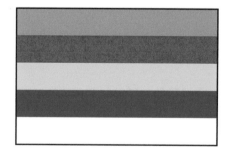

Druze

Flags Of The World

East Timor

East Turkestan

Easter Island

Ecuador

Egypt

El Salvador

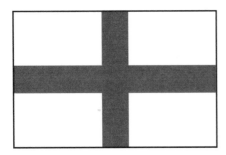

England

Equatorial Guinea

Eritrea

Estonia

Ethiopia

Europe

Flags Of The World

Falkland Islands	Faroe Islands	Fiji

Finland	France	French Guiana

  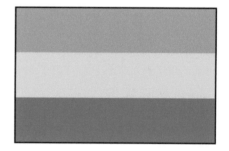

French Polynesia	French Southern	Gabon

  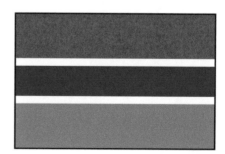

Gagauzia	Galmudug State of Somalia	Gambia

Flags Of The World

Garifuna

Georgia

Gambier Islands

Germany

Germany

Ghana

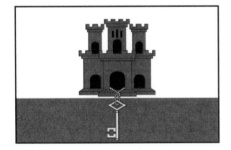

Gibraltar

Gilgit
Baltistan

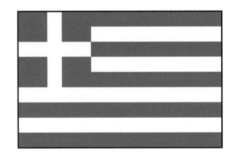

Greece

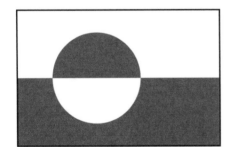

Greenland

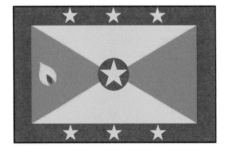

Grenada

Guadeloupe

Flags Of The World

Guadeloupe

Guam

Guambiano

Guatemala

Guatemala
(indigenous)

Guernsey

Guinea

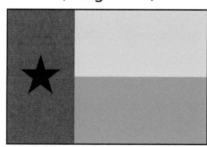

Guinea-Bissau

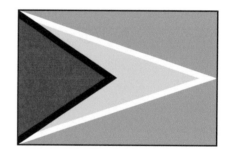

Guyana

Haiti

Haudenosaunee

Hawaii

Flags Of The World

Honduras

Hong Kong

Hungary

Iceland

India

Indonesia

Iran

Iraq

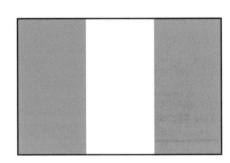

Ireland

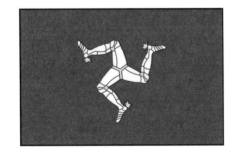

Isle of Mann

Israel

Italy

Flags Of The World

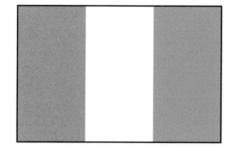
Ivory Coast

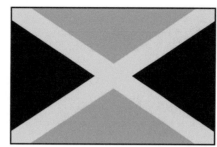
Jamaica

Jammu and
Kashmir

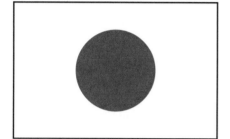
Japan

Jersey

Johnston Atoll

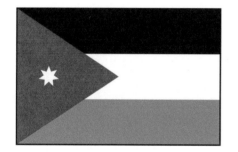
Jordan

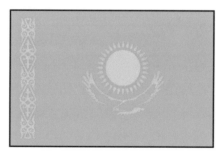
Kazakhstan

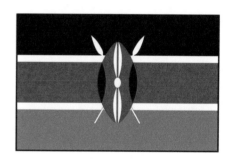
Kenya

Kiribati

Kosovo

Kosrae

Flags Of The World

Kurdistan

Kuwait

Kyrgyzstan

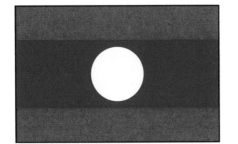

Laos

Latvia

Lebanon

Lesotho

Liberia

Libya

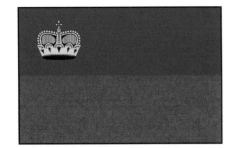

Liechtenstein

Lithuania

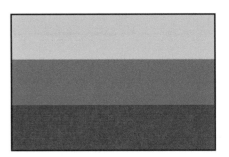

Lithuania

Flags Of The World

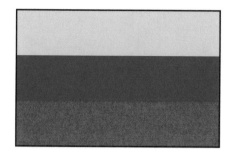 Lugansk Republic

 Luxembourg

 Macau

 Macedonia

 Madagascar

 Madeira

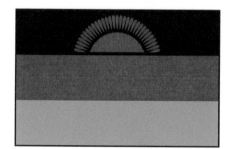 Malawi

 Malaysia

 Maldives

 Mali

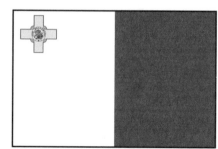 Malta

 Māori

Flags Of The World

Mapuche

Marquesas Islands

Marshall Islands

Martinique

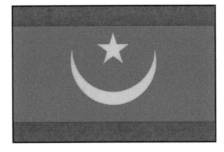

Mauritania

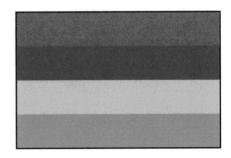

Mauritius

Mayotte

Melilla

Métis

Mexico

Micronesia

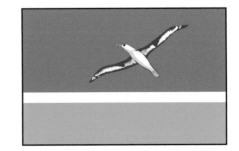

Midway Islands

Flags Of The World

| Moldova | Monaco | Monaco |

  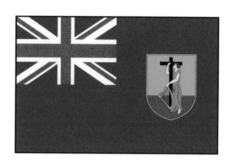

| Mongolia | Montenegro | Montserrat |

 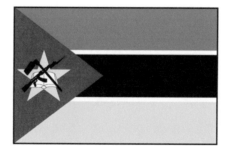 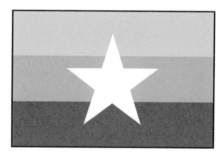

| Morocco | Mozambique | Myanmar |

 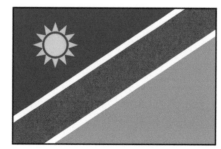 

| Nagaland | Namibia | NATO |

Flags Of The World

Nauru

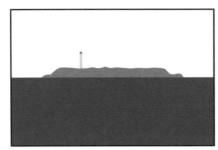

Navassa Island

Navajo

Nepal

Netherlands

Netherlands
Antilles

New Caledonia

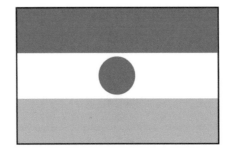

New Zealand

Nicaragua

Niue

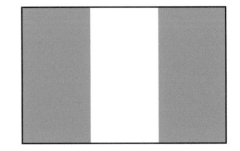

Niger

Nigeria

Flags Of The World

Norfolk Island

North Korea

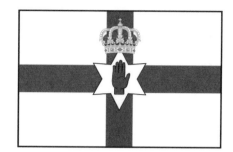

Northern Ireland

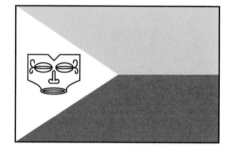

Northern Mariana

Norway

Novorussia

Ogoni

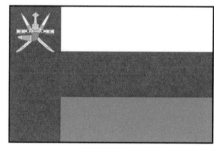

Oman

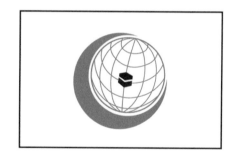

Organization of
Islamic Cooperation

Oromia

Pakistan

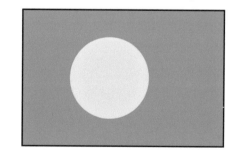

Palau

Flags Of The World

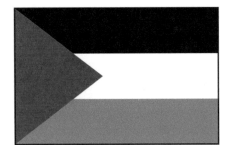

Palestine

Palmyra Atoll

Pan-African

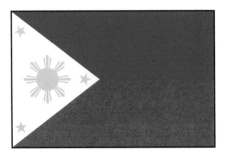

Papua New Guinea

Paraguay

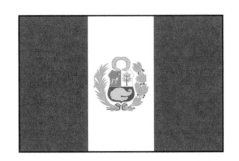

Peru

Philippines

Pitcairn Islands

Pohnpei

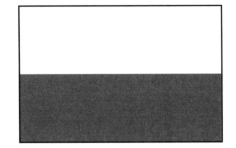

Poland

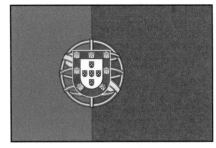

Portugal

Puerto Rico

Flags Of The World

Puntland

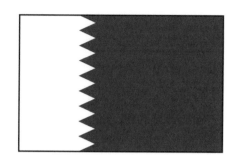

Qatar

Quebec

Quechua

Rohingya

Romani

Romania

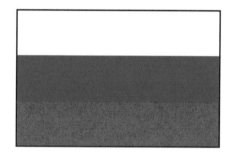

Russia

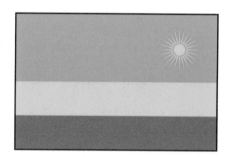

Rwanda

Saba

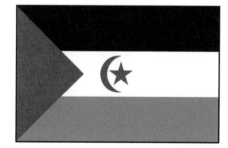

Sahrawi Arab DR

Saint Barthelemy

Flags Of The World

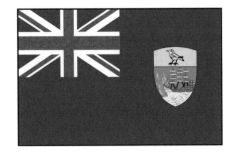

Saint Helena

Saint Kitts and Nevis

Saint Lucia

Saint-Martin

Saint-Pierre and Miquelon

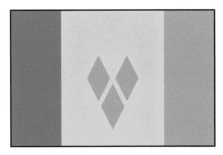

Saint Vincent and the Grenadines

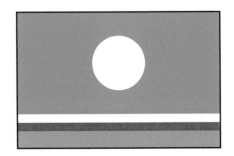

Sakha

Samoa

San Marino

Sao Tome and Principe

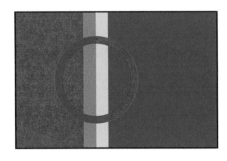

Sápmi

Saudi Arabia

Flags Of The World

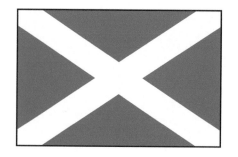

Scotland

Senegal

Serbia

Seychelles

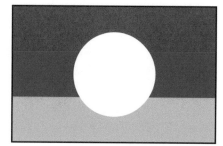

Shan

Sicily

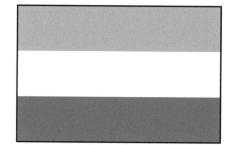

Sierra Leone

Singapore

Sint Eustatius

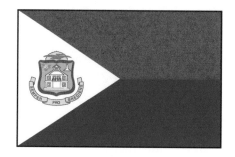

Sint Maarten

Slovakia

Slovenia

Flags Of The World

Solomon Islands

Somalia

Somaliland

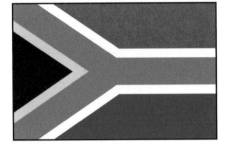

South Africa

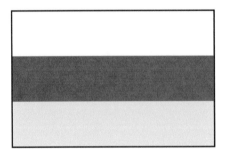

South Georgia

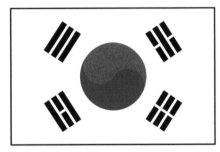

South Korea

South Sudan

South Ossetia

Spain

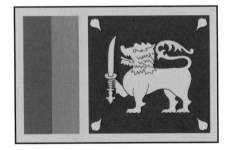

Sri Lanka

Sudan

Suriname

Flags Of The World

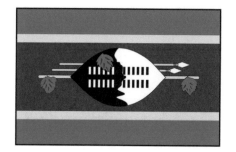

Swaziland

Sweden

Switzerland

Syria

Syria opposition

Taiwan

Tajikistan

Tanzania

Tatarstan

Thailand

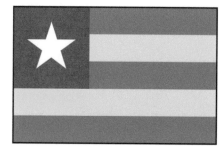

Togo

Tokelau

Flags Of The World

Tonga

Torres Strait Islander

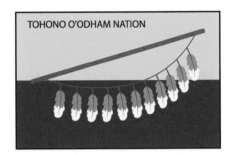

Tohono O'odham

Transnistria

Trinidad and Tobago

Tristan da Cunha

Tunisia

Tuamotu Islands

Turks and Caicos Islands

Turkey

Turkish Republic of Northern Cyprus

Turkmenistan

Flags Of The World

Tuvalu

Tyva

Udmurtia

Uganda

Ukraine

United Arab
Emirates

United Kingdom

U. S. Virgin Islands

United States
of America

Uruguay

Uzbekistan

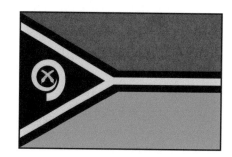

Vanuatu

Flags Of The World

Venezuela

Vietnam

UNASUR

UNIA

United Nations

Wake Island

Wales

Wallis and Futuna

Wallonia

Western Sahara

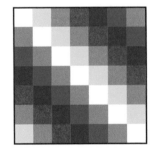

Wiphala

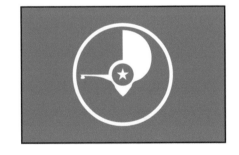

Yap

Flags Of The World

Yemen

Zambia

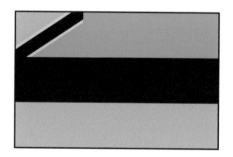

Zanzibar

Zimbabwe

Flags Of The World

My address is posted for you to send pictures , dancing, different foods recipes different things that's going on in your part of the world.

Address:

P.O. Box 628 Hemingway

South Carolina 29554

americasblessedchildren@gmail.com

Name:

Address:

Phone number:

Other books by this Author:

Kalip Adventures

London Alphabet Puzzle

London Number Puzzle

Come Home to Africa